THE APPLE IS EVERYTHING

Barnaby Barford

ACC ART BOOKS

To the apple,

Humble yet mighty, you have permeated every corner of our culture and civilization since the dawn of society!

You are Adam & Eve, the Judgement of Paris and Heracles. You are Cezanne and Magritte, you are Newton, Alan Turing and Steve Jobs. You are Snow White, William Tell and The Beatles, the Viking Gods and the American frontier.

You have been a symbol of peace, love and immortality but also poison and death.
You have tempted us. You have given us youth, knowledge and power, you have shown us sin and you have shown us redemption.

You have been there in all our stories, sometimes as an extra but often as the protagonist.

Adam & Eve had everything, but there you were tempting them to want MORE. Was it knowledge or was it freedom?

In another time, in another guise, dressed in gold and inscribed with 'To The Fairest' you were unwittingly the cause of the Trojan War after the Judgement of Paris.

You were the prize when Heracles outwitted Atlas. You were also used as a decoy in a running race, tricking Atalanta into falling in love with Hippomenes.

It wasn't only the Greeks who saw your power. You kept Odin, Thor and the other Viking Gods forever young.

You have been a muse to artists throughout the ages. Caravaggio, Picasso, Lichtenstein. Lalanne, Matisse and McCarthy. "Be an apple!" Cezanne would implore to his sitters. "You wretch! You've spoiled the pose. Do I have to tell you again you must sit like an apple? Does an apple move?!"

You have led me to discover such great delights as Tal Shochat's tree photographs where every fruit and leaf is immaculately polished. I have fallen for William Mullan's most enchanting photographs of you. I have found Gu Dexin's incredible installations and wish I could experience the full sensory overload that must exist in the sight and smells as you rot.

It is not only the art world you have touched but that of science too. You inspired Isaac Newton to unravel the theory of gravity. It was also you whom Harold Edgerton chose to shoot with a bullet in the most fantastical of photographs, the first man to harness electricity to freeze time to an instant. Tragically, you were also said to have poisoned master codebreaker Alan Turing.

We have bobbed for you on Halloween and we have used your peelings in search of our destiny in love. You 'tamed' the American frontier as settlers planted orchards of saplings sold by the infamous Johnny Appleseed. You kept them in good spirits with cider, yet, always malleable, you promised them good health during Prohibition.

In China you are, by dint of a play on words, a symbol of Peace, given as presents at Christmas time.

You were responsible for Yoko Ono and John Lennon falling in love. You have been sculpted and dried into dolls' heads and you once had a fight with Dorothy and the Scarecrow.

You have been a bad apple, a rotten apple, you have upset the applecart on which you stand. You have never fallen far from the tree, you have been a lump in my throat and you are also one of the biggest cities on Earth.

You have not only touched me, but countless others throughout time. You have inspired us, pulled us up to greatness and taken us to the darkest depths of humanity.

Even when you were most likely a fig or a quince, or even an orange, we called you an 'Apple'.

So, whether you are a Golden Delicious, a Pink Lady or a completely sour inedible cider apple…

I love you.

Barnaby
xx

a is for apple

illustrated by LYNN N GRUNDY

Ladybird Books

Apple Records – All Rights of the Manufacturer and of the owner of the Recorded Work Reserved

(7YCE.21542)
R 5898

Startling
Music
Essex Int.
MCPS
Britico
NCB

℗ 1971
Mfd. in U.K.

45 r.p.m.

Produced
by:
GEORGE
HARRISON

An E.M.I.
Recording

IT DON'T COME EASY
(Richard Starkey)
RINGO STARR

Unauthorised Public Performance, Broadcasting and Copying of this Record Prohibited

Charles Apple

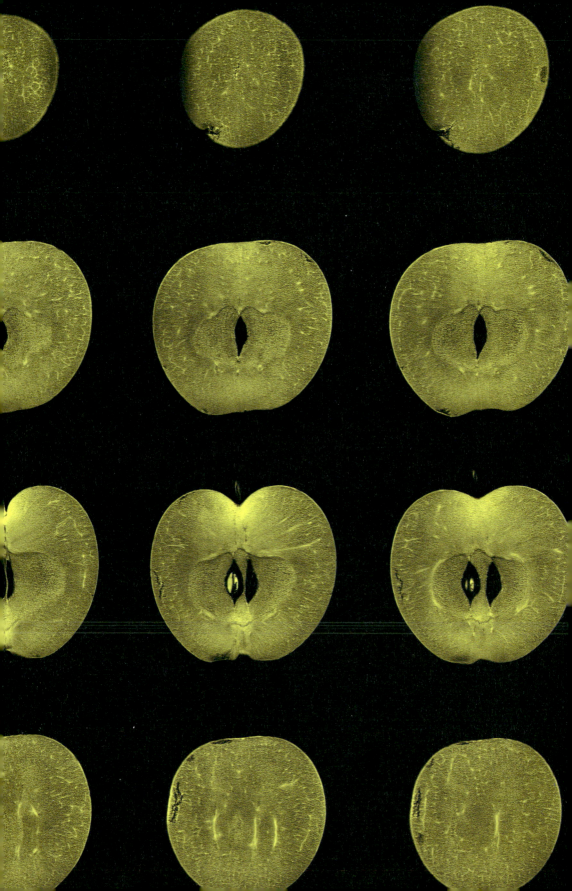

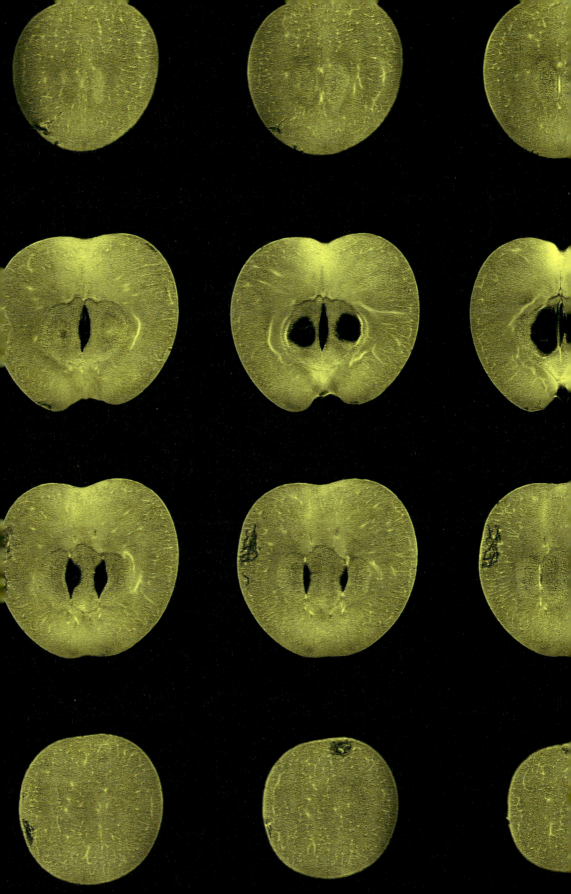

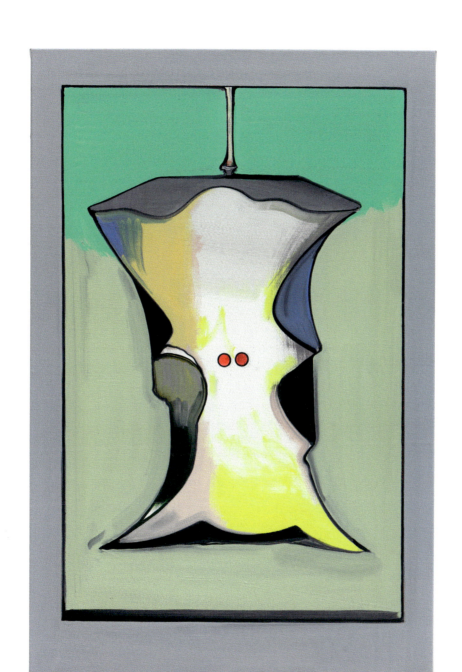

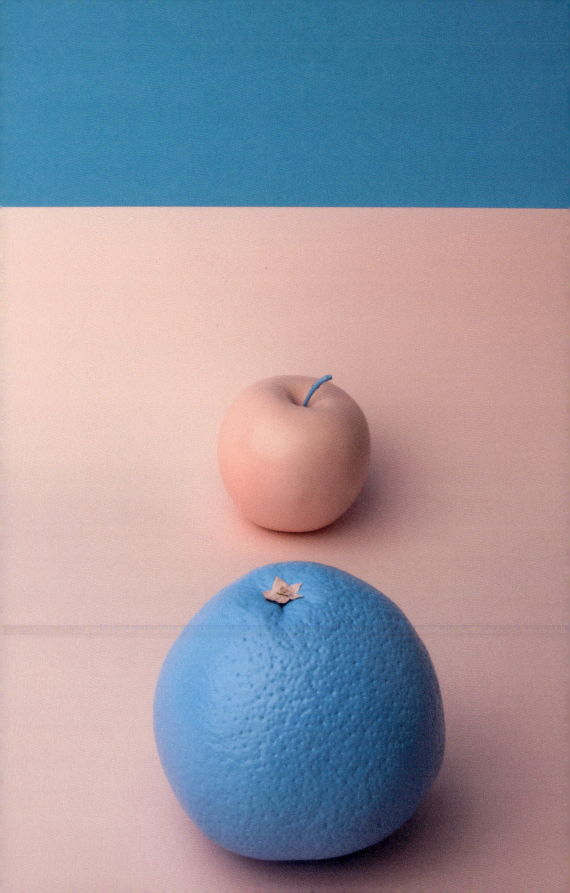

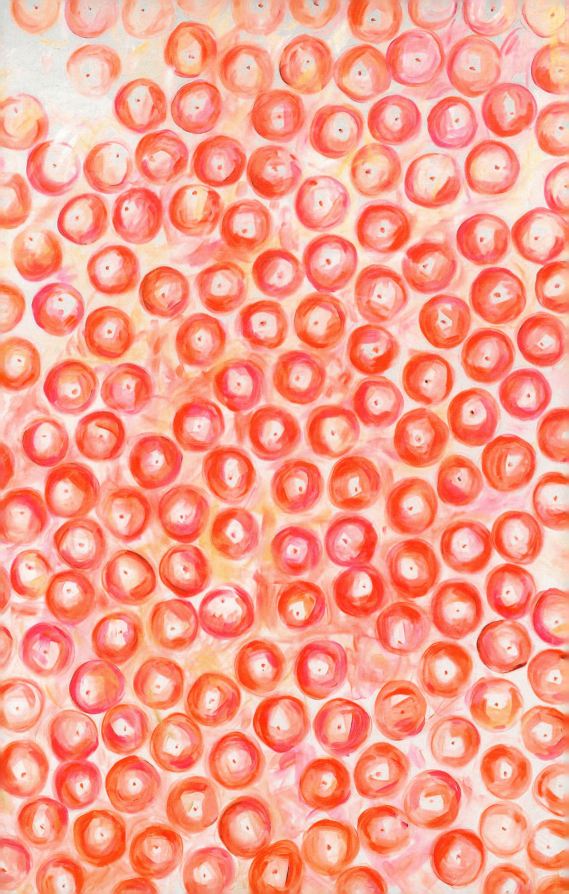

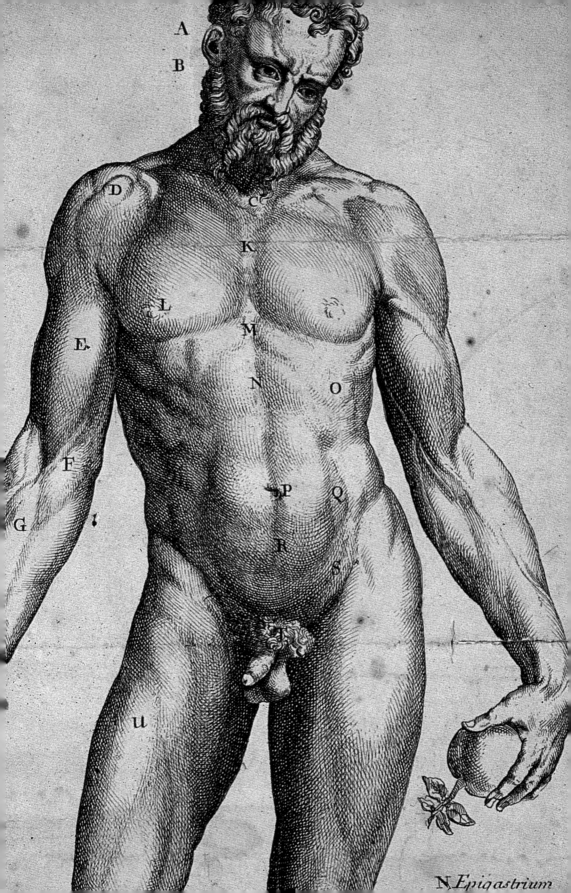

N.Epigastrium

TOMBER DANS LES POMMES*

GEEVESTON FANNY
GRIMES' GOLDEN
GROSEILLE
GRANNY SMITH FLAT
FRENCH CRAB
GOLDEN NOBLE
GRAND DUKE CONSTANTINE
GOLDEN PIPPIN
GROS DOUX
GOLDEN HARVEST
GRANNY SMITH
GEORGE NELSON
GOLDEN SWEET
GEORGE CARPENTER
GOLDEN DELICIOUS
JUBILEE

Herr Zirkel spazieret hin und her,
Den Kopf von großen Ideen schwer.

Plötzlich sieht er voll Verlangen.
Einen reifen Apfel hangen.

Und siehe keine Minute entflieht,
Als den Apfel vom Baume er fallen sieht.

Wie groß vom Baume der Abstand ist,
Der Doctor mit dem Zirkel mißt.

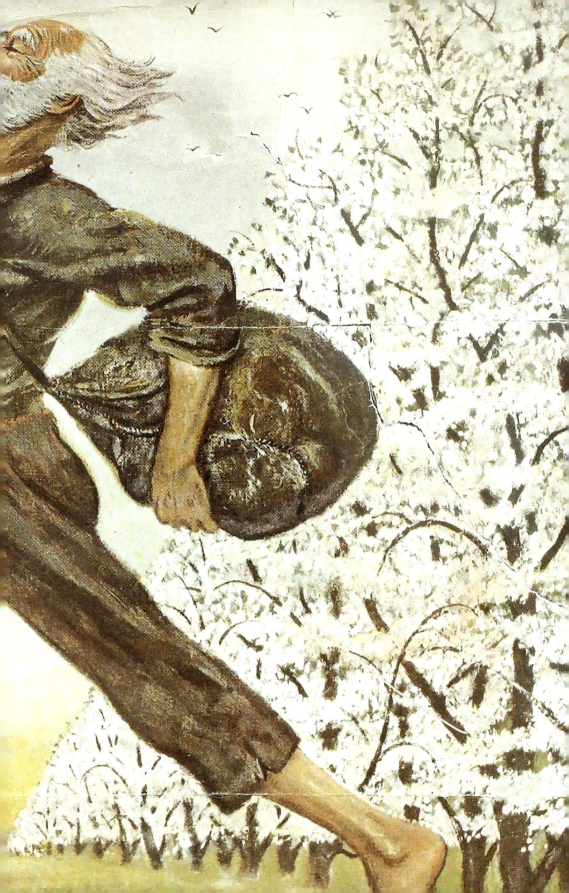

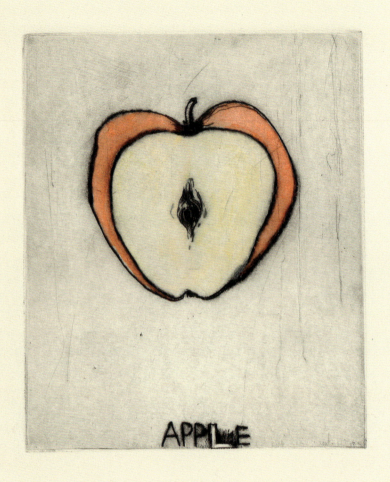

BULMERS STRONGBOW CIDER

SERVE CHILLED

RAUCH

APPLE
JUICE

عصير تفاح

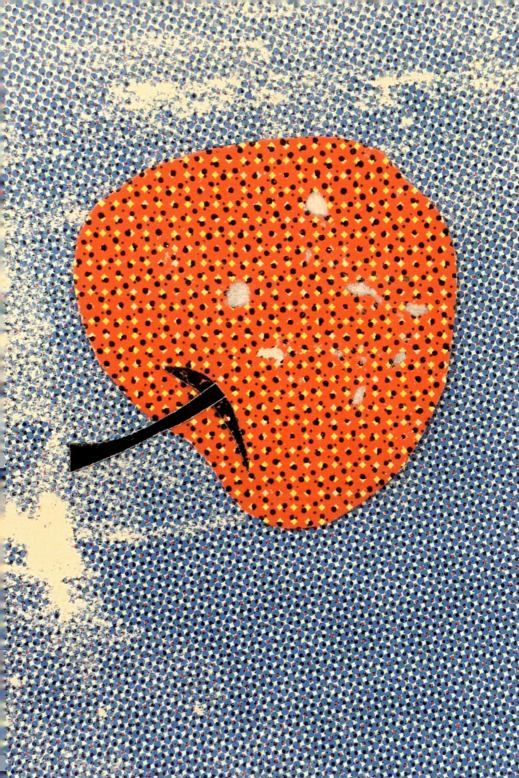

Drink.

And I a glass of cider, just
To help make some one bad.

ATX 2012 APPLE VARIETIES

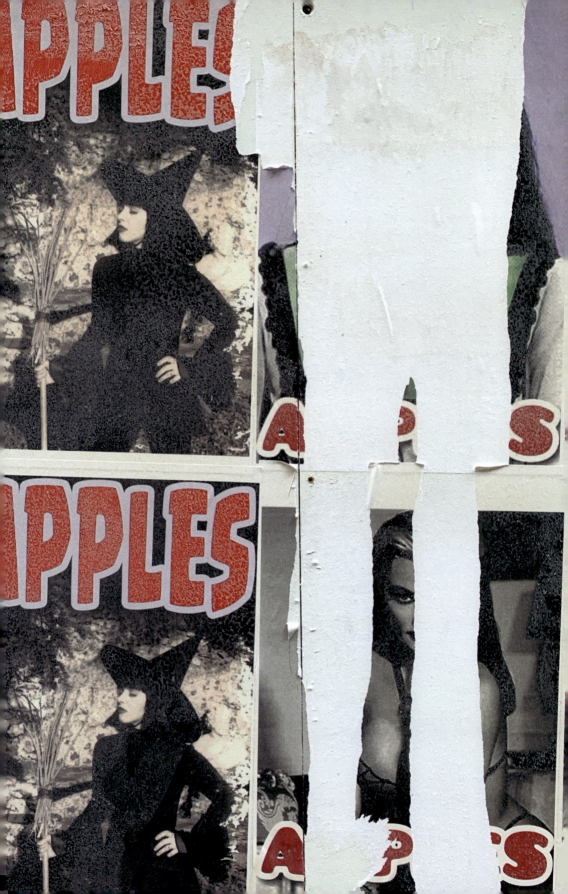

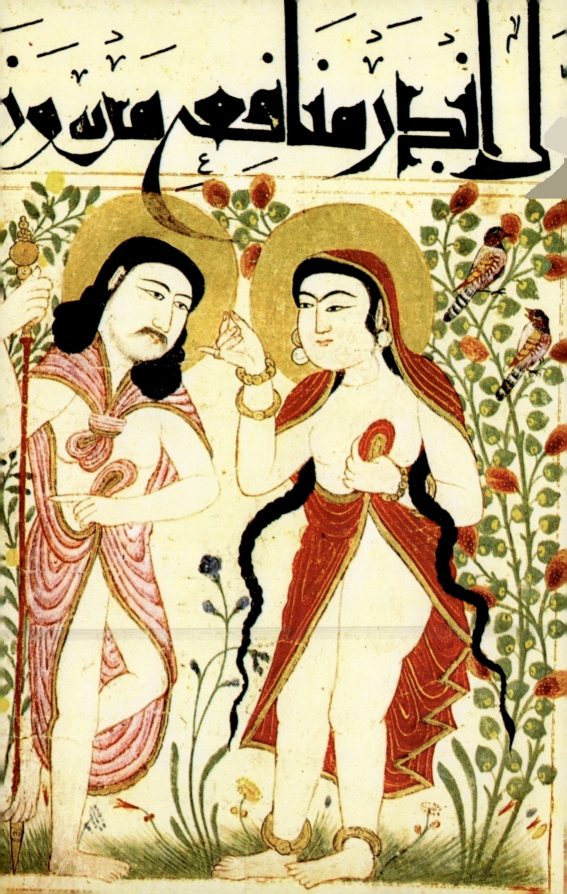

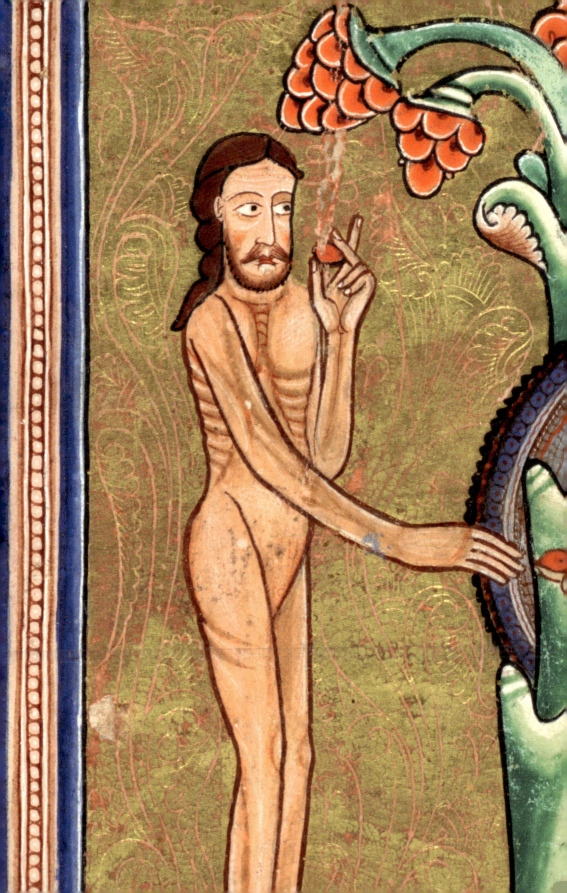

UNEMPLOYED

BUY APPLES

5c. EAC[H]

N.º 109. Reinette rouge.
wiegt 9. Loth Anf. May.

N.º 112. Rothstriemigte Reinette.
wiegt 5. Loth
End. May.

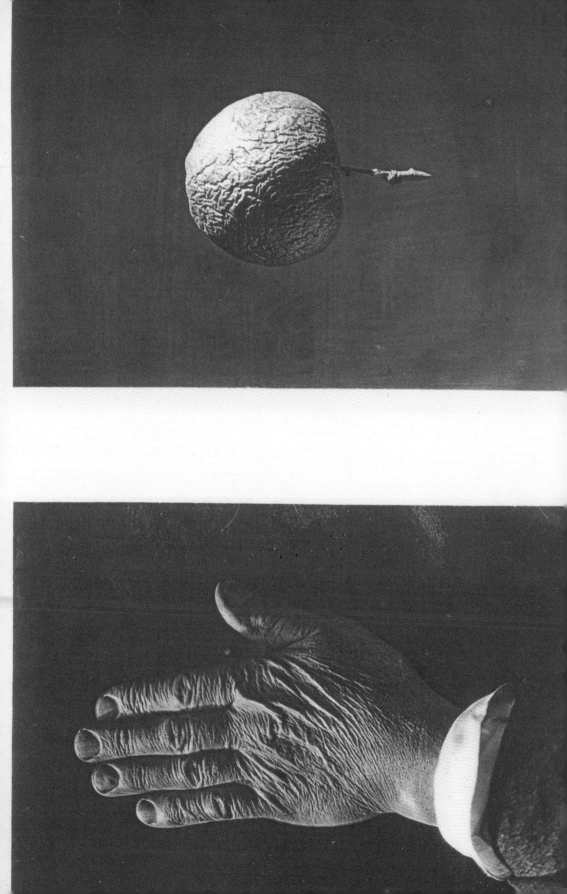

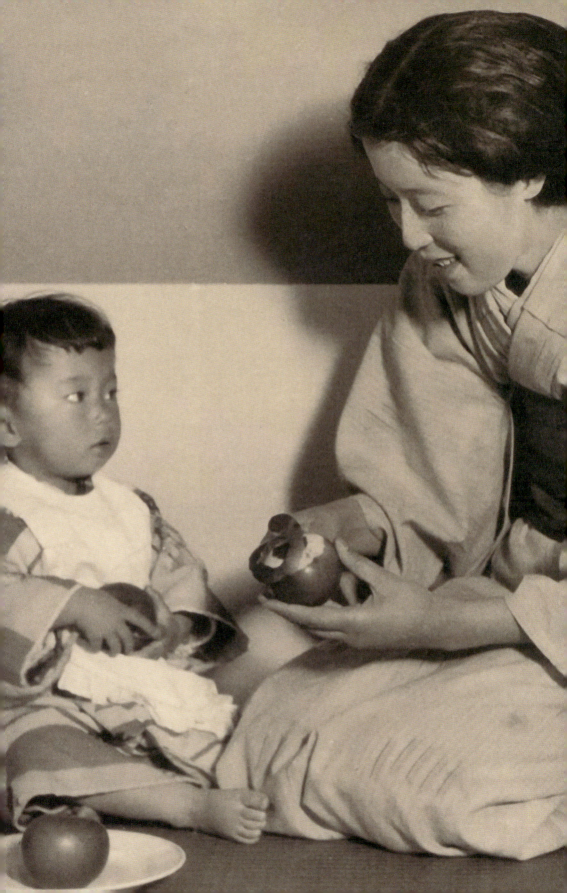

Double Apple Palette with g

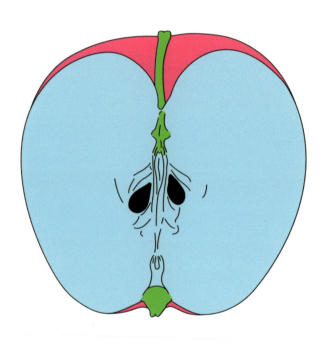

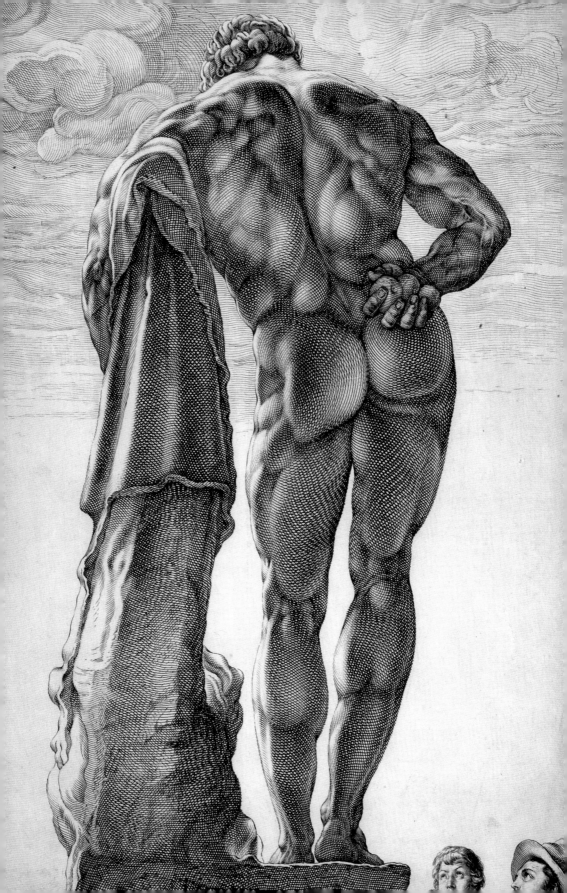

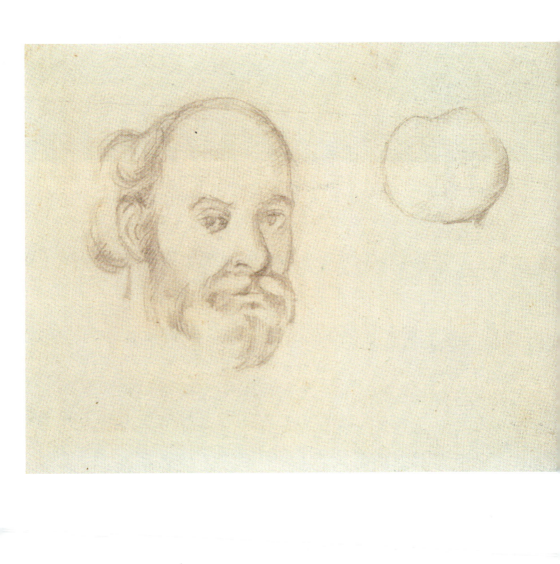

rst teeth are important

If they are lost too soon
there won't be enough space
r second teeth to come through properly.

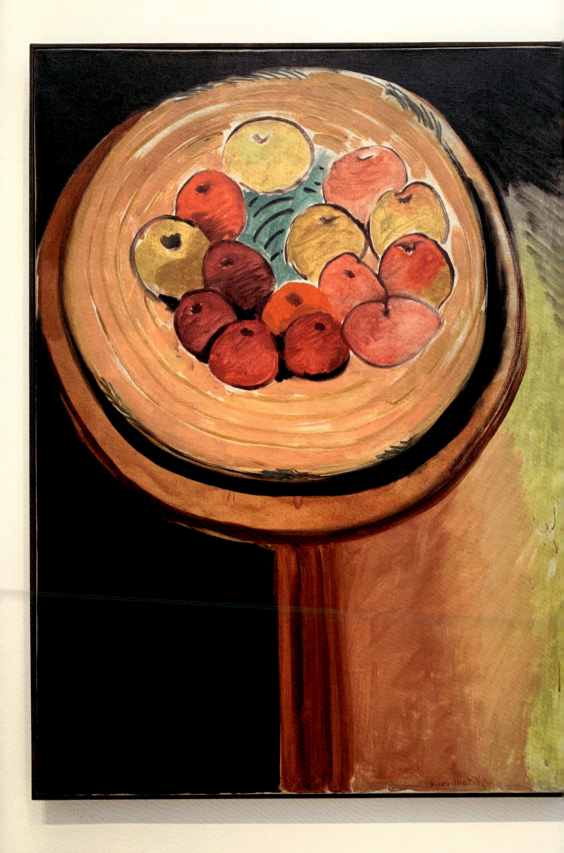

Natürlich.

mach's mi

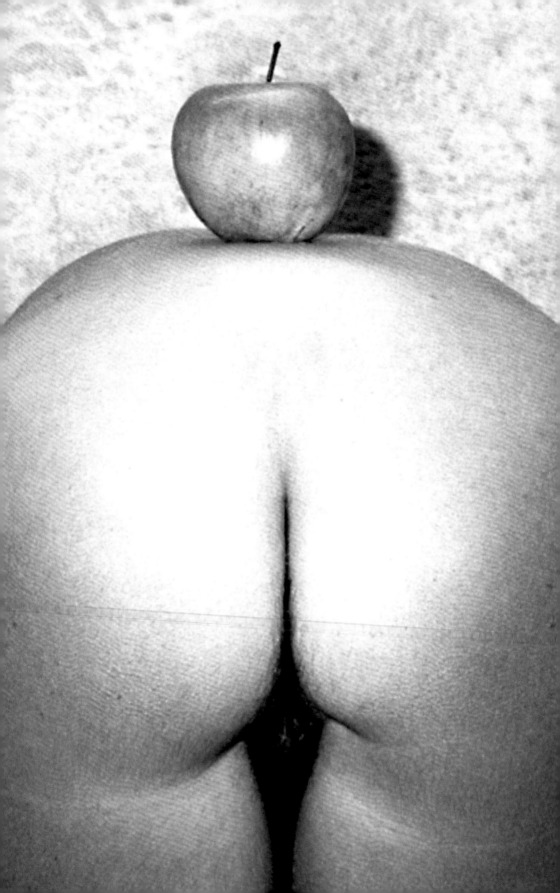

Quick new way to make grand apple pie

Just add sugar and water to **Apple Pyequick!**
Choice apple slices, spice, pie crust mix...all in 1 package

Betty Crocker of General Mills says:

"ake homemade apple pie s new, far easier way"

don't peel apples! Simply empty the ry, ready-to-use apple slices and into a bowl. The apples quickly re to their original natural orchard ness when you add water.

don't cut in shortening! Pie crust mix es practically ready to roll out. r the apples, pour juicy filling into ; top with tender pastry. Pie's in oven in 14 minutes!

A Winesap

ine getting choice pie apples NOW! can—in Apple Pye*quick*. About 2 of tart, firm, fresh-flavored varieties eeled, cored, sliced and quick-dried ach package.

To make a long story short—use Apple Pye*quick*! Takes just half the time to make apple pie this easy new way. And what a pie it is . . . tender, tart apples, delicately spiced and sugared—between two flaky crusts.

Who could ask more of an apple pie? thing is—even *now* when choice pie a season, you can make this delectable pie with Apple Pye*quick*. Pick up a

Apple Pyequick apple pie in a pack

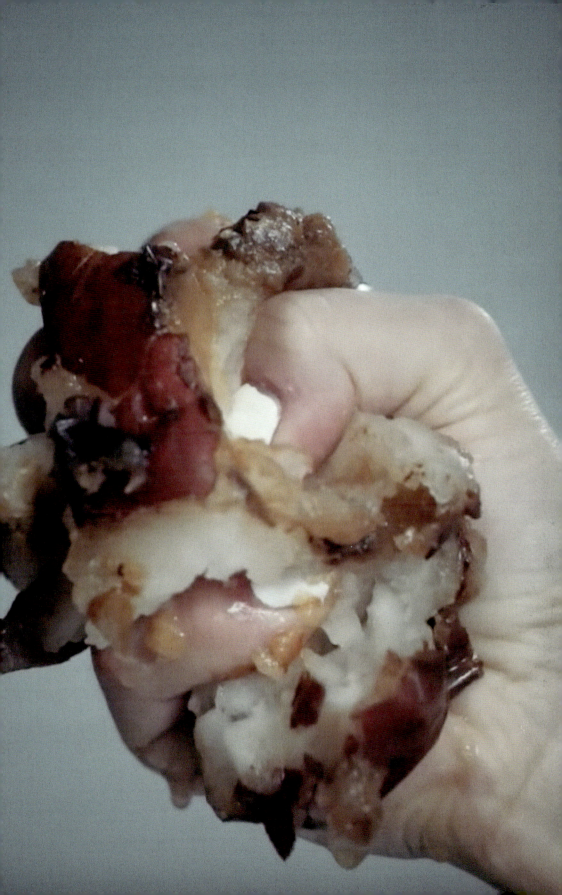

YOU MAY LIKE

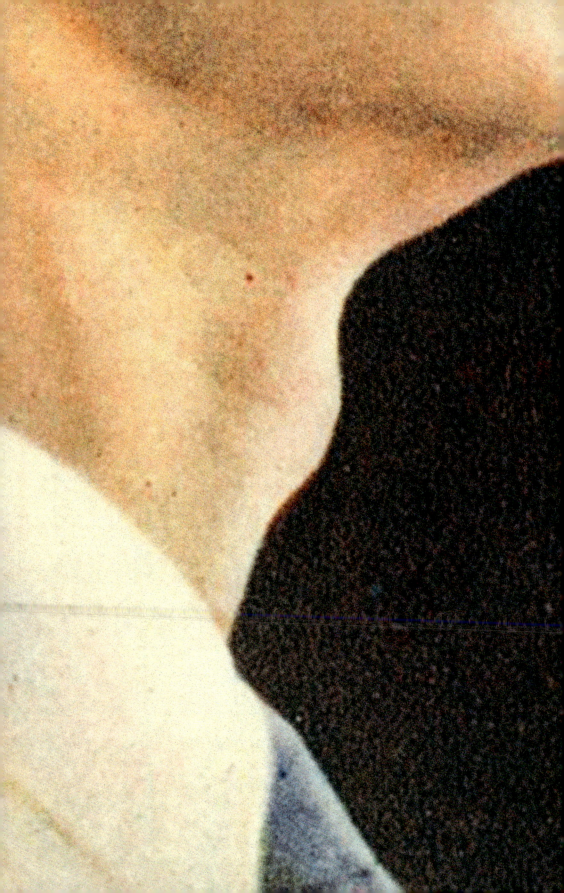

end pages	Rembrandt van Rijn, Adam and Eve (detail), 1638. Etching. Collection and image credit: Rijksmuseum, Amsterdam
6	Yoko Ono, Apple, 1966. Plexiglas pedestal, brass plaque, apple. Photo by Ian Macmillan © Yoko Ono
7	From A is for Apple by Illustrated Copyright Lynn N Grundy, published by Ladybird Books. Reproduced by permission of Penguin Books Ltd. ©
8	Albrecht Dürer, Adam & Eve (detail), 1507. Oil on panel. Collection: Museo Nacional del Prado, Madrid
9	Caravaggio, Basket of fruit (detail), c. 1597 - 1600. Oil on canvas. Collection: Veneranda Biblioteca Ambrosiana, Milan
10	Lucas Cranach the Elder, Adam (detail), 1528. Oil on panel. Collection: Galleria degli Uffizi, Florence. Bridgeman Images
11	Man Ray, Cine-Sketch: Adam and Eve (Marcel Duchamp and Bronia Perlmutter), 1924. Gelatin silver print ©Man Ray Trust / Artists Rights Society (ARS), New York / ADAGP, Paris
12	Painting of Adam and Eve inside Abreha and Atsbeha Church, Ethiopia
13	Paul Gauguin, Self-Portrait with Halo and Snake (detail), 1889. Oil painting on wood. Collection: National Gallery of Art, Washington, D.C.
14	René Magritte, Ceci n'est pas une pomme (This is not an apple) by Magritte, René François Ghislain (1898-1967) Oil on masonite/Surrealism/1964/Belgium/Private Collection/agefotostock © Fine Art Images © ADAGP, Paris and DACS, London 2022
15	Ringo Starr - It Don't Come Easy, 1971, 7" single on Apple Records. TheCoverVersion / Alamy Stock Photo
16	Roy Lichtenstein, still life with portrait from 'Six Still Life' (detail) 1974. © Estate of Roy Lichtenstein / DACS
17	August Macke, Portrait with Apples (Portrait of the Artist's Wife) (detail), 1909, Oil on canvas. Collection: Lenbachhaus, Munich
18	Michael Craig-Martin, iPhone 6s, (detail) 2015. Digital print on Hahnemühle photo rag bright white. Courtesy Michael Craig-Martin and Cristea Roberts Gallery
19	Four cultivars of apple (Malus pumila cv.), c. 1820. Coloured etching. Wellcome Collection, London
20/21	Claude Lalanne, Pomme de New York, 2006. Bronze. © Claude Lalanne, Courtesy of Domaine du Muy. Photo by JC Lett. © ADAGP, Paris and DACS, London 2022
22	Figurine, made of papier mâché, in the form of a skeleton seller of toffee apples. Collection: British Museum, London © The Trustees of the British Museum
23	Lucas Cranach the Elder, Eve (detail), 1528. Oil on panel. Collection: Galleria degli Uffizi, Florence. Bridgeman
24	Vera Chytilová, Daisies, 1966. Film still © DACS 2022
25	Jessie Wilcox Smith, plate from 'Snow White - A Child's Book of Stories' (detail), Chatto & Windus: London, 1 British Library
26	Paul Cezanne, The Plate of Apples (detail), c.1877. Oil on canvas. Collection: The Art Institute of Chicago, IL
27	Frederick Schiller. William Tell, 1952. Classics Illustrated No.101. Illustrated by Maurice Del Bourgo
28/29	H.H. Blakesly, Newtown Pippin Apples, c. 1925. Gelatin silver print. © 2022. Digital image, The Museum of Modern Art (MoMA), New York/Scala, Florence
30	Our Apples are Wild, designed by Bart Sasso (Sasso & Co) for Shacksbury Cider
31	Michelangelo Pistoletto, La mela reintegrata, 2014 - 15. Silkscreen on supermirror stainless steel. 30 x 40 cm. Courtesy Cittadellarte - Fondazione Pistoletto, Biella. Photo by A. Lacirasella
32	German Lorca, Eating Apple (Comendo maça) (detail), 1953. Gelatin silver print. Collection: MoMA, New York Digital image, The Museum of Modern Art, New York/Scala, Florence
33	Ford Madox Brown, Mauvais Sujet, 1863. Watercolour on paper. Collection: TATE, London
34/35	Albrecht Dürer, Adam & Eve (detail), 1504. Engraving. Collection: The Metropolitan Museum, New York, NY
36	Anthony Van Dyck, The Shepherd Paris, 1628. Oil on canvas. Collection: The Wallace Collection, London
37	Peter Hujar, Forbidden Fruit (David Wojnarowicz Eating an Apple in an Issey Miyake shirt) from The Twelve Per Christmas Gifts from Dianne B. portfolio, 1983. Gelatin silver print © 2021 The Peter Hujar Archive / Artists R Society (ARS), New York
38	Joachim Patinir, Temptation of St Anthony (detail), circa 1515. Oil on panel. Collection: Museo Nacional del Prado, Madrid
39	Gustaf Tenggren Book illustration. Snow White and Witch with Poisoned Apple, 1937. © Disney
40/41	Gerhard Richter, Äpfel Apples, 1984. Oil on canvas © Gerhard Richter 2021 (0242)
42	Engraving by G.G. Frezza, after C. Maratta, The Judgement of Paris, 1708. Wellcome Collection
43	Barnaby Barford, Even More (still), 2019. Time-lapse 43:14, colour, loop. Courtesy of the artist and David Gill C
44	Michiel Coxie, Original Sin (detail), circa 1510-1550. Oil on panel. Collection: Kunsthistorisches Museum, Vien
45	Barnaby Barford, Even More (still), 2019. Time-lapse 43:14, colour, loop. Courtesy of the artist and David Gill C
46	Bill Brandt, René Magritte with 'The Great War [La grande guerre]', 1946 © ADAGP, Paris and DACS, London
47	Antico (Pier Jacopo Alari Bonacolsi), Paris, ca. 1500–1505. Bronze. Collection: The Metroplitan Museum, New York, NY
48	Medium Trench Mortar from WW1, also nicknamed "Toffee Apple"
49	Peter Paul Rubens (after Titian), Adam & Eve (detail), 1628-29. Oil on canvas. Collection: Museo Nacional del Prado, Madrid
50/51	Hieronymus Bosch (Workshop of), The Temptations of Saint Anthony Abbot (detail), 1510 - 1515. Oil on oak p Collection: Museo Nacional del Prado, Madrid
52/53	Barnaby Barford, This Earth of Majesty, this seat of Mars, 2019. High density foam, fibre glass, oak. Installation view in Holland Park, London. Courtesy of the artist and David Gill Gallery

Children's World - Girls eating apples, 1935-45. New York World's Fair 1939-1940 records, Manuscripts and Archives Division, The New York Public Library

Jean Baptiste Greuze, Boy with an Apple (detail), late-18th century. Oil on canvas. Collection: Detroit Institute of Arts. Peter Horree / Alamy Stock Photo

Anri Sala, Praise the Power, 2017. Ink on stone paper in 2 artist's frames.
17 1/2 x 12 1/8 x 1 1/8 in. (44.5 x 30.8 x 2.6 cm) (each). Courtesy of the artist and Marian Goodman Gallery

Elliott & Fry, Alan Turing, 29 March 1951. Vintage bromide print on photographer's mount.
©National Portrait Gallery, London

Model apple, 1984. Clay, paint. British Museum, London © The Trustees of the British Museum

The son of Swiss folk hero William Tell waits for his father to shoot the apple on his head.
World History Archive / Alamy Stock Photo

Reproduction of the SNB's 50 Franc banknote ('Apple Harvest') (detail), designed by Pierre Gauchat, fifth series, issued in 1957, recalled in 1980. Courtesy SNB Archives

Guido Reni, Hippomenes and Atalanta, 1618 - 1619. Oil on canvas. Collection: Museo Nacional del Prado, Madrid

Jean-Baptiste Regnault, The Judgement of Paris (detail), 1820. Oil on canvas. Collection: Staatsgalerie Stuttgart

Bernardino Luini, Madonna with Child and apple (detail), 1525. Colletion: Gemäldegalerie, Berlin

Glykon, reproduced from the original by Lysippos. Farnese Hercules (detail), c. 216 AD (4th century BC for original). Collection: Museo Archeologico Nazionale, Naples

Carlo Crivelli, Virgin and Child (detail), ca. 1480. Tempera on panel.
Collection: Victoria and Albert Museum, London

Isaac Newton (detail), picture from Meyers Lexicon books, 1905-1909. Nicku / Shutterstock

Boys scrumping apples from a tree (detail), c. 1800. Chronicle - Alamy Stock Photo

Wilhelm Engelhard, Idunn with Apples of Immortality (detail), 1857, from the Edda Frieze. Photo by Ernst Alpers

Cherry Yoshitake attempting to break a Guinness World Records title for the 'Most apples bobbed in one minute (37)'.
© Guinness World Records

© Aino Kannisto, Untitled (Apple Tree) (detail), 1997. Courtesy Galerie m, Bochum, Germany

Mark Gertler, The Artist's Brother Harry Holding an Apple (detail), 1913. Oil paint and tempera on wooden panel.
Collection: TATE, London

Gerbrand van den Eeckhout, Portrait of a Six-Year-Old Boy Holding an Apple (detail), 1656. Oil on canvas.
Collection: Agnes Etherington Art Centre at Queen's University, Ontario

Apple, sagittal view, MRI. Credit- Alexandr Khrapichev, University of Oxford. Wellcome Collection, London

Billy Apple®, NZ/USA, CUT, 1964. Offset lithography on T.H. Saunders paper. Printed by Roy Crossett.
Courtesy of The Mayor Gallery, London

Vincent Price holding a shrunken head, 1975

Greek Silver Coin, 560-546BC. British Museum, London © The Trustees of the British Museum

William H. Martin, A Load of Good Iowa Apples, 1909, Gelatin silver print. © 2022. Digital image, The Museum of Modern Art, New York/Scala, Florence

Gu Dexin, September 2nd 2006, 2006, Installation. 5 tons of apples, bulldozer, variable dimensions. Courtesy: Artist and GALLERIA CONTINUA, San Gimignano / Beijing / Les Moulins / Habana / Rome Photo Oak Taylor-Smith

Francks Deceus, Apple Pie #4, 2005, Mixed media on canvas, 61 × 76.2 cm. Courtesy of the artist and Arco Gallery

Roy Lichtenstein, Apple Badge, 1966. © Estate of Roy Lichtenstein/DACS 2022

Thomas Scheibitz, Apfel, 2017. Oil, vinyl and pigment marker on canvas. 120 × 80 cm. Private collection Heidelberg.
Courtesy: Thomas Scheibitz & VG Bild Kunst. Photo: Gunter Lepkowski

Glass model of an apple (Malus pumila) with apple scab caused by the fungus Venturia inaequalis. Model number 813, Rudolf Blaschka, 1932. Credit Line: The Ware Collection of Blaschka Glass Models of Plants, Harvard University Herbaria/Harvard Museum of Natural History. Photo by Jennifer Berglund ©President and Fellows of Harvard College

Tal Shochat, Blacks and Reds, 2004, c-print, 120x120 cm Courtesy of the artist and Rosenfeld Gallery

Franz Juttner, The Queen has poisoned Snow White, 1905. Illustration from Sneewittchen, Scholz' Künstler-Bilderbücher, Franz Jüttner, 1905. Historic Images / Alamy Stock Photo

The Judgement of Paris, artist unknown

Barnaby Barford, Adam & Eve, 2011, Found porcelain figures, 2 way mirror, light fitting, resin.
Courtesy of the artist and David Gill Gallery

André Britz, Colour Fruits, Colourmorphology

Camille Pissarro, Apple Harvest at Eragny (detail) 1888, Oil on canvas. Collection: Dallas Museum of Art, TX

Jutta Koether, Pink Ladies 3, 2019. Oil on canvas. 63 x 82 11/16 inches (160 x 210 cm).
Photo: Dario Lasagni. Private Collection USA

William Mullan, Niedzwetzkyana. Photograph. Courtesey of the artist

Michiel Coxie, The Holy Family (detail), 1540. Oil on panel

Lucas Cranach, The Judgement of Paris (detail), 1530-35. Oil on Panel. Collection: Windsor Castle

Terry Evans, Untitled (detail), from the Kansas Documentary Survey Project. 1974. Gelatin silver print, mage: 7 × 7 in. (17.8 × 17.8 cm). Collection: Smithsonian American Art Museum, Washington DC. Courtesy of the artist. 2021 ©Photo Smithsonian American Art Museum/Art Resource/Scala, Florence

Egon Schiele: Seated Boy Holding Apple (Anton Peschka, Jr.). 1917. Gouache, watercolor, and black crayon.
Private collection. Image courtesy Kallir Research Institute, New York, NY

A male nude, seen from the front, holding an apple (detail), early 18th c. Engraving after a woodcut from 1543.
Wellcome Collection, London

106	Pablo Picasso, Still Life with Pitcher and Apples, 1919. Oil on canvas Photo ©Photo Josse / ©Succession Picasso/ DACS, London 2022 / Bridgeman Images
107	Vertumnus, Roman mosaic (detail). Late 2nd century AD. Roman period. Limestone and marble. Collection: Museu Arqueológico Nacional, Madrid
108	Junsuke Yokoyama, Apples II, 2019. Paper, clay, acrylic color, polyvinyl chlorides. Courtesy if the artist
109	Ringo Starr of The Beatles samples an apple during a visit to Australia House in London, England - 22 Apr 1964 AP Photo/Shutterstock
110	Artwork (detail) for the Andy Partridge EP recording Apples & Oranges/Humanoid released, 2018 by Ape House Artwork by Andrew Swainson from an idea by Andy Partridge © Ape House Ltd.
111	APPLE. Learning to Design, Designing to Learn © Ken Miki
112	Zelda Zonk, Tomber dans le apples, 2020 © Zelda Zonk/TV5Monde
113	Jack Pulman, The Happy Apple, 1970. Programme cover for The Apollo Theatre, London
114	Cornelis Bisschop, Woman Peeling an Apple (detail), 1667. Oil on panel. Collection: Rijksmuseum, Amsterdam
115	Pascal Malepo Wiemers. www.selam-x.com. Courtesy of the artist
116	Willie Smith's Apple Shed Museum in Tasmania
117	Doctor Zirkel follows Newton's famous steps under the fabled apple tree (detail). Coloured wood engraving. Collection: Wellcome Collection, London
118	Barnaby Barford, This nurse, this teeming womb of royal kings, 2022. Bronze with silver nitrate patina. Courtesy of the artist and David Gill Gallery
119	Barnaby Barford, This nurse, this teeming womb of royal kings, 2022. Bronze with silver nitrate patina. Courtesy of the artist and David Gill Gallery
120	Hans Eworth, Elizabeth I and the Three Goddesses (detail), 1569. Oil on panel
121	Arik Levy, Mineralized Painting (Apples on a Tree), 2012. Print and acrylic paint on composite board. www.arik Photo: Ian Scigliuzzi
122	Albrecht Dürer, Adam & Eve (detail), 1507. Oil on canvas. Collection: Museo Nacional del Prado, Madrid
123	Claude Lalanne, Pomme Bouche, Designed 1975 © ADAGP, Paris and DACS, London 2022
124	Deirdre McKenna, The Fortress, 2012. Brass, apple on plinth. Courtesy of the artist © Deirdre McKenna
125	Enzo Mari with Elio Mari, The Nature Series, No. 1: the apple, 1961. Silk-screen print on texilina paper
126	René Magritte, The Postcard, 1960. Oil on canvas. © ADAGP, Paris and DACS, London 2022
127	Barnaby Barford, Paris Pavement, 2019
128	Barnaby Barford, To the fairest, 2019. Coloured pencil on paper. Courtesy of the artist and David Gill Gallery
129	Constantine Dako (Κωνσταντίνος Ντάκο), Paradise lost, 2019. Traditional ink on heavy cotton paper.
130	Cesar Boetius Van Everdingen, Boy Holding an Apple (detail), 1664. Oil on canvas. Collection: Cannon Hall Museum, Cawthorne
131	Ugo Rondinone, still.life. (apple), 2008 © Ugo Rondinone, courtesy Sadie Coles HQ, London
132/133	Kashmiri farmers pack fresh apples in an organic orchard on 1 October 2018. ZUMA Press, Inc. / Alamy Stock
134/135	Cerise Doucède, EGAREMENTS (detail), 2010. Photograph. Courtesy of the artist
136	Paul Cézanne, The Basket of apples (detail), c. 1839. Oil on canvas. Collection: The Art Institute of Chicago, Il
137	Anya Gallaccio, Because I Could Not Stop, 2002 Direct-cast bronze, ceramic, rope. © Anya Gallaccio. All Rights Reserved, DACS/Artimage 2022
138/139	An illustration in The Saturday Evening Post showing American folk hero Johnny Appleseed is part of the collec at the Johnny Appleseed Educational Center and Museum at Urbana University, OH
140	'What to Eat' poster, designed and printed by Banning Press. St. Paul, Minnesota, USA, c.1905. ©Victoria and Albert Museum, London
141	B25 Apple wallpaper, designed by William Morris in 1877, printed by Jeffrey & Co. before 1940. Courtesy Willia Morris Gallery, London Borough of Waltham Forest
142	William Mullan, Peau d'Ane. Photograph. Courtesy of the artist
143	Neil Phillips, Green Man (from the Mendip Morris Men) celebrating the Wassail at Thatchers Cider in Somerset
144	Jim Dine, Apple from These Are Ten Useful Objects Which No One Should Be Without When Traveling, 1961. One from a portfolio of ten drypoints with gouache additions © 2021 Jim Dine / Artists Rights Society (ARS), N York Apple. © 2022. Digital image, The Museum of Modern Art, New York/Scala, Florence
145	Charlotta Janssen, Intertwined Adam and Eve Leaning on Apple Tree (detail), 2016. Iron Oxide, Acrylic, Collage & Oil Varnish
146/147	Edvard Munch, Adam and Eve (detail), 1909. Oil on Canvas. Collection: Museo Thyssen-Bornemisza, Madrid
148	Vintage can of Bulmer's Strongbow cider (detail)
149	Vintage can of a RAUCH Apple juice (detail)
150	Boy with Apple by Johannes Van Hoytl (the younger) (detail). Credit: Fox Pictures
151	Robert Gober, Melted Rifle, 2006. Plaster, paint, cast plastic, beeswax, walnut and lead. 27 1/8 x 23 x 15 3/4 inches. 69 x 58 x 40 cm.© Robert Gober, Courtesy Matthew Marks Gallery
152	Barnaby Barford, New York, 2018. Photograph
153	Apple Pickers (detail).
154	Jacques Chirac puppet made by Les Guignols
155	Apple seeds, botanical illustration
156	Barnaby Barford, Rotting Apple 3, 2019. Photograph
157	Alfred Stieglitz, Georgia O'Keeffe (detail), 1924. Gelatin silver print. Collection: Philadelphia Museum of Art,

George Mnyalaza Milwa Pemba, Young Couple (detail), 1949. Oil on canvas. Image Courtesy Leonard Joel
Barnaby Barford, Untitled, Collage, 2018
AnnMarie Breen, Apples blown from trees in orchard used by Bulmers Cider in Tipperary Ireland during Storm Ophelia, 2017
Marcus Coates, Apple Service Provider, 2018. Photography by Ken Adlard Commissioned by Hauser & Wirth Somerset for the exhibition 'The Land We Live In – The Land We Left Behind', curated by Adam Sutherland
Edward Carswell, Food not Drink, Temprances Stories and Sketches, originally from Carswell 'Pen and Pencil; or Pictures, Puzzles, and Short Stories for Boys and Girls' (New York: The National Temperance Society and Publication House, 1890). Courtesy Oshawa Museum
Bill and Beverly Niffenegger, Apple Boy, 2010. Roadside mascot for emporium & bistro in High Rolls, New Mexico. Franck Fotos / Alamy Stock Photo
Bartolomeo Bimbi, Mele (detail), 1696-99. Villa di Poggio a Caiano, Prato
Alison Turnbull, Colour Chart ATX2012 (Apple Varieties), 2012. Archival inkjet print 420 x 297 mm. Courtesy of the Artist and Matt's Gallery. All rights reserved, DACS 2022
Howard Cook, Portrait of B, 1928. Etching on paper. Collection: Smithsonian American Art Museum, Washington, D.C. © 2022 Photo Smithsonian American Art Museum/Art Resource/Scala, Florence
Hiram Powers, Cast of the Right Arm and Hand of "Eve Tempted" (little finger missing), n.d. plaster and metal. Collection: Smithsonian American Art Museum and its Renwick Gallery, Washington, D.C.
The Wizard of Oz, 1939. Film still. Everett Collection Inc / Alamy Stock Photo
Petra Collins, Roza with Apple (detail), 2016. Courtesy the artist
Jeffery Edwards, Work, 1972. Screenprint on paper. Collection: TATE, London.
Eleanor Antin, Judgement of Paris (after Rubens) (detail), 2007, from "Helen's Odyssey". Chromogenic print, 38 x 73 inches, edition of 5 © Eleanor Antin
Apple Tree Wassail Score
Sarah Illenberger, Hairy Apple (Fashion Fruits), 2015. Fine Art Print. 40 X 60 CM. Limited Edition of 100 + 5 AP
William Hunt, Apples (detail), unknown. Watercolour. Collection: TATE, London
Street poster. Photo by Barnaby Barford
Andy Warhol, Apple, 1983. Synthetic polymer paint and silkscreen ink on canvas © 2022 The Andy Warhol Foundation for the Visual Arts, Inc. / Licensed by DACS/Artimage, London
A Christmas apple seller in China
Adam and Eve (detail), 1294–99. Painting from Manafi al-Hayawan (The Useful Animals) from Maragheh, Iran
Illuminated Manuscript (detail), 18th century Ethiopian Vellum, tempera, and leather binding. Collection: Princeton University Art Museum, NJ
Adam & Eve (detail), c. 1170. Miniature from 'The Hunterian Psalter'. Courtesy University of Glasgow Library, Archives & Special Collections
Oskar Laske, Happy Apple Harvesting (detail), ca. 1925. Watercolor and gouache on paper. © courtesy Kovacek & Zetter, Vienna
throwingsofas, Is that an apple?! 2016. Jackson, OH
James Gillray, The Tree of LIBERTY (with the devil tempting John Bull) (detail), 1798. Etching on paper
Miniature from the Codex Aemilianensis, Adam and Eve and the Tree of Good and Evil (detail), 994. Collection: Royal Library of San Lorenzo de El Escorial, Madrid
Paul Barnett with his unique apple tree, which has 250 different varieties of apples growing on it - 23 Sep 2013. M Y Agency/Shutterstock
Jane Alden Stevens, A farmer in Japan uses a wand to pollinate each blossom by hand. © 2010 Jane Alden Stevens
Picture of the Cider museum's yard when it was an orchard. Coloured photograph. Courtesy of Hereford Cider Museum Trust
James Gillray, The Apples and the Horse-turds, or Bonaparte among the Golden Pippins (detail), published on 24 Feb 1808.
Unemployed: Buy apples 5 cents each (detail). 1930. Rare Books Division, The New York Public Library
Bert Hardy, Untitled (Child with Toffee Apple) (detail). ca. 1950. Silver gelatin print
Will Barnet, Ruth Bowman (detail),1967. Oil and graphite on canvas, 114.3 x 60.3 cm. Collection: The Metropolitan Museum of Art, New York, NY © Will Barnet Foundation, Courtesy Alexandre Gallery, New York © 2022 Image copyright The Metropolitan Museum of Art/Art Resource/Scala, Florence
Fall Games – The Apple-Bee (detail). Wood engraving in black ink on paper published on the Harper's Weekly, November 26, 1859. Collection: Cooper Hewitt, Smithsonian Design Museum, New York, NY
Gabriël Metsu, A Woman Seated at a Window (detail), early 1660s. Oil on wood. Collection: The Metropolitan Museum, New York, NY
Andy Sweet, Man with Apple: Garden of Eden (detail), 1979. Vintage Print. Courtesy Andy Sweet Photo Legacy
Barnaby Barford, Untitled, 2020
Bronzino, Venus, Cupid, Folly, and Time (detail), c. 1545. Oil on wood. The National Gallery, London
Johann Hermann Knoop, Illustration from Pomologia Book Nurberg, 1760
Urs Fischer, A-Z, Cast bronze, acrylic primer, gesso, oil paint. Installation view at Gagosian 2020. Photo by Barnaby Barford ©Urs Fischer
Correggio, Assumption of the Virgin (detail), 1526-1530. Fresco inside Parma Cathedral
Mangzi Tian, Astrological phase, 2003. Courtesy of the artist

204	Master of the Legend of Mary Magdalen, Madonna and Child (detail), unknown. Oil and gold ground on panel. Courtesy Koller Auctions Ltd., Zurich
205	Barnaby Barford, Apple, 2019. Photograph
206	James Nasmyth. Back of Hand & Shrivelled Apple. To illustrate the origin of certain mountain ranges by shrink the globe, c. 1870. Two Woodburytypes on a lettered sheet. Collection: Rjiskmuseum, Amsterdam
207	Antony Gormley, ONE APPLE, 1982 Apples, lead and air 7 x 1110 x 7 cm (53 pieces altogether) © the artist
208	Yang Guang, Green Apple (detail), 2013. Electronic chips. Courtesy of the artist and Linda Gallery
209	Japanese unknown artist, Mother and Son (detail), c. 1932. Photograph. Collection: Philadelphia Museum of A
210/211	Jim Dine, DOUBLE APPLE PALETTE WITH GINGHAM, 1965. Lithograph and fabric collage on East Indian made paper. 23 5/8 x 28 inches. Courtesy Jim Dine Studio and Gray, Chicago/New York
212	Michael Craig-Martin, Naked Apple, 2012. Archival inkjet print. Courtesy Michael Craig-Martin, Large Glass, London and Fondación Helga de Alvear, Cáceres, Spain.
213	Barnaby Barford, Tom in his apple tree, 2019. Photograph
214	Inagaki Tomoo, Abstract Still Life with Apple and Grapes (detail), ca. 1948. Woodblock print. Courtesy Scholten Japanese Art, New York
215	William Blake, The Judgement of Paris (detail), 1806-17. Watercolour. Collection: The British Museum, London
216	Zhanna Kadyrova, APPLE, 2010. Concrete, cement, brick wall fragments, porcelain tile. 300 x 300 x 300 cm. Courtesy of the artist
217	Limbourg Brothers,Très Riches Heures du duc de Berry, 1411-1416. Tempera on Vellum, Illuminated Manuscrip Collection: Condé museum
218/219	Samira Makhmalbaf (director), The Apple (original title: Sib), 1998. Film still. Photo 12 / Alamy Stock Photo
220/221	Barnaby Barford, Truth & Lies Apples, 2019. Oil paint on bone china. Courtesy of the artist and David Gill Gal
222	Anne Rook, 4021, Golden Delicious Apple (sweet and crunchy). From a series of 4021 & 4020 Golden Delicious Apples. Inkjet Print on blueprint paper © 1999, 2002, 2003 Anne Rook
223	Hendrick Goltzius, Farnese Hercules (detail), 1592, dated 1617. Engraving. Collection: The Metropolitan Museum, New York, NY
224	Bernard Fleetwood-Walker, The Family (detail), oil on canvas. © the estate of Mrs P. Fleetwood-Walker. Photo Courtesy: The Potteries Museum & Art Gallery
225	US stamp honoring Johnny Appleseed, 1966. Designed by Robert Bode and issued at Leominster, Massachusetts
226	Hugh Steers, Mouse & Apple (detail), 1988, Oil on board, 26 × 27.9cm © ARS, NY and DACS, London 2022
227	Yinka Shonibare, Adam and Eve, 2013. Installation view at Blain Southern, photo by Christian Glaeser ©Yinka Shonibare CBE. All Rights Reserved, DACS 2022
228	Paul McCarthy, Apple Heads on Swiss Cheese, 1997-1999. 2 parts: fiberglass, silicone, Ed. 2/3, 370 x 190 x 150 cm / 145 5/8 x 74 ¾ x 59 inches. Ursula Hauser Collection, Switzerland © Paul McCarthy. Courtesy the artist and Hauser & Wirth
229	Apple pie makes you sterile, Badge, 1960-80. Plastic-coated offset lithograph on paper mounted on metal disc
230	Paul Cèzanne, Self portrait with Apple, 1882-3. Graphite on paper
231	American fruit lover Michael Goudeau attempting to break a Guinness World Records title for the 'Most bites ta from three apples whilst juggling in one minute'. © Guinness World Records
232	Eduard Lebiedzki, Judgement of Paris (detail), 1906. Oil on canvas
233	Study for Fruit Bowl (with Apple), Ettore Sottsass, aerial perspective, 1973. © 2022. Digital image, The Museum Modern Art, New York/Scala, Florence
234	Will you have an Aomori apple (detail) © Aomori Prefectural Museum
235	CIBO, Untitled, 2022, spray on wall, size 1.5 x 5m, Verona, Italy
236	Lucas Cranach, The Virgin and Child Under an Apple Tree (detail), c. 1530. Oil on canvas. Collection: The State Hermitage Museum, Saint Petersburg
237	Dental hygiene; showing a toddler and his teddy bear in a high chair on which are placed a carrot and an apple (detail). ca. 1960. Colour lithograph. Wellcome Collection, London
238	Ute Doll from Utah (detail), circa 1915. Courtesy of Theriault's
239	Jiri Kolar, Mona Lisa Apple, 1963. Collage on found object, ebony. © Jiri Kolar - Heirs
240	John F. Francis, Still Life (detail), Apples and Chestnuts, 1859. Oil on panel. Collection: LACMA, Los Angeles,
241	Circle of Michel Erhart, Christ Child with an Apple (detail), ca. 1470–80. Willow with original paint and traces gold. Collection: The Metropolitan Museum, New York, NY
242	Henri Matisse, Still Life with Apples, 1916. Oil on panel. Collection: Chicago Art Institute, IL. ©Succession H. Matisse/ DACS 2022
243	Russian street apple seller pre-1900. The Keasbury-Gordon Photograph Archive. KGPA Ltd / Alamy Stock Phot
244	Guido Meyer and Marcel M. Kolvenbach. Poster for the >Join In< campaign, 1993. Colour lithograph. Courtes the artists, BZGA, and Wellcome Collection, London
245	Mercury (Hermes) offering a golden apple to Paris (detail). Etching by P. Aquila after Annibale Carracci. Collection: Wellcome Collection, London
246	Camille Pissarro, Apple Picking, (detail) 1886. Oil on canvas. Collection: Ohara Museum of Art
247	Mathys Schoevaerdts, The Game With The Apple (detail), between 1682 and 1702. Etching and engraving. Collection: Rijks Museum
248	Kahn & Selesnick, "Garrett, Queen Anne's Lace, Apple", 2016. Courtesy of the artists

Unknown Netherlandish artist, John Bourchier, 2nd Baron Berners (detail), circa 1520-1530. Oil on panel. Collection: National Portrait Gallery, London
Andrew Sietsema, Ghost apples, 2019
Rotten Apple, 2019. Photo by Barnaby Barford
Nicolas Colombel, Atalanta and Hippomenes (detail), c. 1680. Oil on Canvas. Collection: Liechtenstein Museum
Barnaby Barford, Falling Apple, 2018. Video still

55 Barnaby Barford, The Apple Tree, 2019. Installation view at David Gill Gallery, London
57 Fabrice Hyber, Impossible 100 pommes 1000 cerises (detail), 2006 © ADAGP, Paris and DACS, London 2022
Marcel Mariën, Le Verger (The Orchard), 1985. Silver print on original mount 23.8 × 17.8 cm. Courtesy Foundation Marcel Mariën © DACS 2022
Barnaby Barford, Royal Gala, 2019. Photograph

61 William Tell, c. 1850. Pen-and-ink lithograph, coloured.
©Collection particulier, AKG Berlin / Pictorial Press Ltd / Alamy Stock Photo
A 1950's Betty Crocker advertisement for Apple Pyequick. Retro AdArchives / Alamy Stock Photo
Pussy Riot & Dave Sitek, Bad Apples, 2018. Video still. Courtesy of the artists
Raphaelle Peale, Still Life with Cake (detail), 1822. Oil on panel. Collection: Brooklyn Museum, New York, NY
John Dilnot, Bad Apples (detail), 2010. Wood, paper, acrylic and glass. Private collection
John Baldessari, Adam wasn't into It, 2018. 10 color screenprint. 33 x 28 in. (83.8 x 71.1 cm). Edition of 50. Courtesy of the artist, Gemini G.E.L. and Marian Goodman Gallery © John Baldessari. Courtesy Estate of John Baldessari
Kehinde Wiley, PORTRAIT OF A VENETIAN AMBASSADOR, AGED 69, II, (detail) 2006. Oil on canvas. ©Kehinde Wiley

69 Maurice Denis, Homage To Cezanne, 1900, Oil on canvas. Collection: Musée d'Orsay
71 John Deare, Judgment of Jupiter, 1786-87. Marble relief. Los Angeles County Museum of Art, LA
How did the 'Adam's Apple' get his name? Cigarette Card. George Arents Collection, The New York Public Library
Pieter Coecke van Aelst's studio, Fall of Man, 1525. Oil on panel. Collection: Dulwich Picture Gallery, London
Raphael, Three Graces (detail), 1503-05 Oil on panel. Collection: Château de Chantilly
John Currin, Maenads, (detail) 2015. Oil on canvas, 48 x 36 x 1 1/4 inches, 121.9 x 91.4 x 3.2 cm. © John Currin. Courtesy Gagosian.
De Scott Evans, Two Hanging Apple, 1890. Oil on canvas. Collection: Yale University Art Gallery, CT
François Joullain, Apple Seller (detail), 1746. Etching with some engraving. Collection: The Metropoliotan Museum, New York, NY
Luca Giordano, Judgement of Paris (detail), 1681- 83. Oil on canvas. Collection: Hermitage Museum, St. Petersburg
Anselm Feuerbach, The Judgement of Paris (detail), between 1869 and 1870. Oil on canvas. Collection: Kunsthalle Hamburg

81 Harold E. Edgerton, Bullet through Apple (detail), 1964 © 2010 MIT. Courtesy of MIT Museum
ages Your Apple Here
Jobless New Yorkers sell apples on the pavement during the Great Depression, New York, USA (detail), 1930. Heritage Image Partnership Ltd / Alamy Stock Photo

I would like to extend a very special thank you to every artist, designer, photographer, musician, scientist, filmmaker, gallery, foundation and institution that has given me permission to use their image in this book.

An enormous thank you also to Ambra Gattiglia, whose contribution to this book cannot be underestimated. It would not have been possible without her.

I would also dearly like to thank David Gill and Francis Sultana for their continued support and enthusiasm.

© 2022 Barnaby Barford
World copyright reserved

ISBN: 978 178884 164 1

The right of Barnaby Barford to be identified as the author of this work has been asserted by him in accordance with the Copyright, Designs and Patents Act 1988.

All rights reserved. No part of this publication may be reproduced, stored in a retrieval system, or transmitted in any form or by any means electronic, mechanical, photocopying, recording or otherwise, without the prior permission of the publisher.

British Library Cataloguing-in-Publication Data
A catalogue record for this book is available from the British Library

The author and publisher gratefully acknowledge the permission granted to reproduce the copyright material in this book. Every effort has been made to trace copyright holders and to obtain their permission for the use of copyright material. The publisher apologises for any errors or omissions in the text and would be grateful if notified of any corrections that should be incorporated in future reprints or editions of this book.

Printed in Belgium
for ACC Art Books Ltd., Woodbridge, Suffolk, England

www.accartbooks.com

YOUR APPLE HERE